Solace

Mark I. Himelstein

ISBN 0-7414-3170-X

Published by:

INFINITY
PUBLISHING.COM

1094 New DeHaven Street, Suite 100
West Conshohocken, PA 19428-2713
Info@buybooksontheweb.com
www.buybooksontheweb.com
Toll-free (877) BUY BOOK
Local Phone (610) 941-9999
Fax (610) 941-9959

Printed in the United States of America

Printed on Recycled Paper

Published May 2006

Contents

Introduction

Dear Reader,

I began very simply. My heart hurt. Something possessed me and I wrote the poem *I'm Always Alright*.

I suspect it starts this way for many people. I am very grateful for my interest in writing. It is a passion in my life. I wrote about 15 poems in the 1980's. I stopped writing for most of fifteen years and then found my marriage falling apart and once again turned to writing. At first it came slowly and I even forced myself to write a poem every day for a while even if it was something short like haiku. Finally, the rhythm came back and it is now part of my life for good.

Sometimes I write each day and other times it is weeks, but I do write. I love it.

I write for myself. I have always written for myself. I write my feelings. I have little that embarrasses me so I shared my words. My friends and acquaintances liked the words. So I continued to share. For years they have asked me to publish. I had tried submitting early ones in the eighties that were rejected and I resisted further attempts.

Now I find that the publishing world is turned on its ear. Self-publishing and publish-on-demand have changed the world of content delivery and give authors incredible freedoms. The keys to the kingdom are now in the hands of many.

I wrote a technical book and published it through publish-on-demand and thought this would be a good avenue for the other side of my brain as well. So here I am humbly before you, dear reader, with my words.

What will you find inside? I have picked forty plus poems that have given me solace. They are poems that I read and re-read often.

I am not a trained poet with an English degree. I have read some others poetry that I love or am intrigued with like David Whyte, Mary Oliver, and Jane Kenyon but I am not extremely well read in poetry. Some poems reflect my earlier writing and are not on par with my later poems. If you are looking for perfect meter or perfectly worked words, you will not find them here. If you are interested in honesty and feelings, I think you will find solace here by my side.

I divided the book into four sections: Love, Loss, Family, and Self.

Love. Non-familial love. I question as many do whether I have ever really loved anyone. Then I look at the words I have written and know that I must have done so. I don't know why the memory is so elusive or why time undermines my perspective so, but I am glad that I have these words. These words immediately bring back the care, closeness and lust of relationship.

Loss. Is there light without darkness? This section explores some of the pit of despair. For me, night really does represent despair. I am sure that most of these words were written at night. I am not a wallower and do not experience deep lasting lows.

While I know some of these words may be hard to read, I assure you that I believe in the morning and renewed purpose. I make lists and I do, but I also cherish the fact that I felt the pain and could write words about that pain.

Family. I have been blessed with my immediate family. While we have had hardship, we are always there for each other and love each other. This section contains an eclectic set of emotions and experiences but they all contain the same love, respect and affection for my family. At this writing, my grandmother (Nana) is not with us in body. She passed a little while ago at the age of 100. She engendered and exemplified the feeling of family. Each poem in this section, even the ones on hardship, warms my heart.

Self. My family and I went through family therapy when I was a teen. I learned to express my thoughts and feelings. The hardships of my earlier years made me more introspective and more of a self-aware person. This section is born of my early experiences and reflects thoughts along my passage. Reading these poems reminds me of where I have been and where I want to go. It reminds me of my humanity and the humanity of those around me.

I hope these poems bring you solace too.

Writing words,

Mark I. Himelstein

For the Muses

Love

Her hair flowed red and her eyes sparkled. She was
wearing a peasant skirt and a white cotton tank top.
I was head over heels …

Feel (11/83)

I feel freshly kissed,
I feel warm inside,

I felt a friend,
I felt serene,
I felt at ease,
      and then I felt the sun amidst the rain.

I felt reluctant,
I felt you nigh,
I felt scared,
      and then I felt comfortable, just the same.

I felt some thought,
I felt some life,
I felt some love,
      and then I felt some feelings deep.

I feel freshly kissed, …

A composite. I was free and acknowledging both a cry for someone, anyone as well as acknowledging the emotionlessness that could overcome me.

Gentle Soul (5/02)

Sometimes we walk through life
and don't know who we are

Oh gentle soul who crossed my path
Be careful of what you may find
My caring seems enough it seems
But comes from nothing at all

My heart skips beats when you are here
And forgets when you are gone
It dreams of unconditional love
And a saviour to be found

My burden is the truth you see
I must tell you what I am
I still believe that one day
You'll come and lay me bare

But the morning light that brings my mind
Will battle for my soul
I pray thee win oh gentle soul
And set me free at last

I want to dance through life, my friend
And know just who you are ...

We drove through a dank fertile forest and she challenged my vocabulary with the word fecund. I knew then that I was in love ...

Fecund Love (8/03)

Like a forest's eyes
Sun strewn beams penetrate the dark
Waiting for primordial mists to rise up and envelop them
A dance with intoxication for all to see and witnessed
      by G-d

Like a forest's legs
Roots and limbs strong and aching
Outstretched limbs wrapped tightly as life depended on it
Nothing forgotten under a blanket of damp needles and
      twigs

Like a forest's belly
Brimming with sex and creation
Exotic colors and shapes that conspire and inspire the
      glory
Generous acts played out under trees and in fields by
      dark and light

Like a forest's bosom
Joyously feeding its inhabitants
A massive chain where each knows their ambrosia waits
Community built by mutual need where evolution rules
      each day

Like a forest's womb
Filled with life nurturing the future
Seeds and seedlings both afraid and coaxed by fecund
      love
Deliberate steps that remind all of the joy that is the
      adventure of life

She is like a forest …

She knew what I wanted. After reading this one, she called me. She whispered "I am yours ..."

Heart, Mind, and Soul (9/03)

Will I love her heart?
Her love is so, can I receive?
Congruence is such, can I believe?
I feel the flood and dams built tall
Her restraint is so I build my wall
In case, in case the well goes dry
The leap refrained by ropes that cry

Will I know her mind?
Her words to me, can they be real?
She thinks I know, but am I that ideal?
I leave a portion for which I reap
Her fear and love in ground doth seep
In case, in case the crop is light
Save the grain in case of blight

Will I feel her soul?
Her being here, can I so trust?
The essence thrives, can it rise from dust?
A house, a picket built to please
Her faith's foundation is laid with ease
In case, in case of some large storm
Just come inside and just stay warm

A scene of happiness. We all have them in our head. My love of impressionism and my impression of us …

Seurat (9/03)

I have a picture in my head
Of life and how it shall be
Some lazy Sunday afternoon
With you and they and me

I have a picture in my head
Of love's bounty all around
Children, cats and dogs
Me smiling without a sound

I have a picture in my head
Of my love and what she brings
Sustenance and joy till full
And on top of that she sings

I have a picture in my head
Where dots combine for real
To make the life we so want
And give us strength to feel

There is a journal in a spa. These bookends mark what could have been the end and what was a new beginning. Extemporaneous love …

Osmosis (10/03)

Bristling twigs and meandering path
Persevere unto my heart
Finding love then keeping love
Is indeed a godly art.

Osmosis II (12/03)

Full lush leaves and moss covered stones
Speak unto my love
Finding faith then keeping faith
Is a gift from G-d above

Sometimes form precedes content. So is the case here. Contemplating her and my good fortune.

Sonnet I (11/03)

When she was born the angels spoke and said
"G-d's glory for this one, we bless her now
For she shall have no easy road ahead.
She'll mold herself, a better life to vow"
Presence and softness for herself to gain
Those near her life were just a ruse. In time
She would decide she would not be the same
For love she chose, for life she chose to climb
She stood her ground and made a life so fair
The rocks that stood before stood no real
      chance
She made her life by work and love and care
The glory is she taught herself to dance
Surely angels blessed me, thus to confer
None else explains the love I have from her.

The challenge of love. The things we bring. The things we are. Come back to love. Come around …

Come Around (11/03)

I love her so that my heart sings
Like a choir for G-d
Images enter my head
Of words

Riding a stallion bent on life and fury
I hold on knowing
My life depends on
My knowing

The beauty stands in white flowing
Winds whipping her
Hair and cloth
Staring clearly

Is it me she sees or can she know?
Blinded by the past
Hands shading her eyes
Straining

It comes and goes this reality
And I wonder
If time will settle
Upon truth

I barely take a breath as I pass
Hand outstretched for her
She sees it now and I
Come around

Love within the confines of things going well may not
be love at all. Love through good and bad is what I
seek ...

Shake the Ground (3/04)

I do not know what to do
When you are present and loving
     All is right,
We can conquer anything
     We can be and do anything

And then like an earthquake it changes
The timber of your voice
     The direction of your energy
Pulls Terra Firma from beneath my feet

Is this how I am too?
If so, we are more a pair than we know
Just maybe we can find our way together
     That one might hold the ground while the
     other shakes it.

Just maybe that is true love…

She asked to write something sexy and I wrote something smoldering instead. I can remember the heat as I read the words myself ...

Rhythm and Sweat (5/04)

The tingle inside my chest
Betrays the blush I feel
And the sly and shy smile
Reveal some deepened passion
O Raven haired Beauty
How can you ask me to ravage thee?
How can you ask me to write of it?
It is a rite of passage
It is not right anyway
Each moment I reach for the small of your back
And start
Start the dance
Can you hear the music?
Can you feel it tighten its grip upon you?
Sway back and forth
Rhythm and sweat
Balance and form
Taste what I have to give
And I will taste of you
Hand and glove
Against the wall
Dancing in place
The music may finally fade
And yet
It will not stop

Loss

~

I had broken up with her 6 times in two years. The 7th time she broke up with me. I am grateful to her because it was then that I wrote my first poem that a friend of mine calls existential Dr. Seuss …

I'm Always Alright! (9/83)

I think at least once, I think that perhaps,
I'd like to enjoy a total collapse.
My subconscious won't fall without a fight,
And it always says, "I'm always alright!"

When my whole life seems a total bore,
And my father is sick and my mother is poor.
To "How are you?" my answer contrite,
Is, regrettably, that I'm always alright.

When it's not my choice and love comes to loss,
My will builds itself, till again I'm the boss.
Once again it is asked: "How is your plight?"
And still it remains, I'm always alright.

Economics are bad and so is the mood,
The world is in hunger and lacks enough food,
Soon will come war and me asked to fight,
Even then I will answer "I'm always alright".

I think I've been burned and fear has come nigh,
That any other answer would bring no reply.
So when I am asked how I'll be this good night,
I guess I'll just state that I'm always alright.

When you travel alone and leave the ones you love. Paranoia that you might not come back. The ache of not having them with you each day...

She Cried (2/02)

I left today
She cried
"Why must you go?
I'll miss you so"
I need to
I tried
"Do you really?
Will you come back to me?"
She cried
I know
"My heart will always yearn,
And I shall return"
I said
She cried
"I am lucky you want me,
I need that you see"
I sighed
She cried
"Smile princess don't feel alone,
Soon, soon I'll be home"
I cried

She died and I could not feel anything. So I thought about what it would feel like if I lost my own...

Another Day (10/01)

Another day when I look up

The sun is not as bright
the flowers do not reach full bloom
and music cannot sooth

Time goes slower than a snail
work seems unimportant
and plans flee in the wind

Children do not laugh carefree
the food tastes like plain bread
and my bed provides no sanctuary

G-d does not seem in his glory
the rules provide no bounds
and people seem not there

Just another day without you …

She was troubled but she made me feel at a time that I
needed to feel...

Love's Ballet (6/03)

How many times must I die?
I am grateful for I knew not that I could once
Down and up like a roller coaster
You dragged my soul with the wind
I fell accompliced in the act
Wanted to believe you were there
My heart struggled to squeeze blood
Unknowing what would happen
I thought you controlled our destiny
But I am clear that is not so
You are a victim of yourself
So back I go to the castle looking for chain mail
But the gap has been opened
And I shall love again

I left her and she re-engaged me but held me at bay. During the wait, I felt more alone than many other times in my life...

Alone (10/03)

This is what alone feels like...

Coming home at the end of the day
No dog or child waiting to run you down
Knowing no one is there
Doubting if anyone cares

It is like a broad expanse of sky
Where there is no horizon
Feeling like you are no part
Searching for where to start

It is like a pain, no an ache
Deeper inside than could be
Try as you might you cannot place it
Removal would mean you're complicit

It is like a night without sleep
Drying your tears to a pillow's mold
Knowing your heart will not mend
Wondering if it will ever end

This is what alone feels like ...

One can have an effect in the mundane corners of your life. Losing her is anything but mundane.

Missing (10/03)

She is missing from our midst.
I sit reading poetry to myself.
My daughter plays in tub amidst disappearing bubbles.
Bubbles inspired by her.
I wipe the sweat from my brow.
She would ask me why I didn't carry a handkerchief
And I conjure her. A ghost.

Smiles and pounces.
The little girl voice that says she loves me and is happy
Reading aloud and playing cards with no one
Where the smell of lavender haunts me.
I walk around doing the perennial wash and think.
Think of someone who likes to fold.
Happy with her life.

I miss live speak
I miss being loved by her in just the same way.
The challenge to lead better lives
Hope of family renewed,
Her foot tape sits on the counter like a remnant.
Handsoap nearby with no indications
She was here

I am paying and praying
I am meeting her and learning and staying.
Breathe in and smile out. Calming myself
Finding this was a past
Now attempting this moment
Writing these words. yet
She is missing ….

Irony and love like magnets of the same pole trying to
mate …

Enough (11/03)

Why isn't it enough?
My love for you
Your love for me
O'Henry is envious
Our irony

I can't do it for you
I must do it for myself
You need to do it
You can not do it for me

I destroyed the things that brought you comfort
I brought you the things you sought
You woke me up from life's slumber
You teeter upon having me reconstruct a wall

Why isn't it enough?
Our love

Sometimes there is no match possible.
Sometimes love is not enough …

Gammon (5/05)

She throws down the pieces and says let's play
She never thought we would
Would run out of things to say
Never thought we would
Would really have to play
She is fast and leaves me behind in my
      Deliberation
Done with hers she starts on mine and I
      Let her go
It's her game
She doesn't want to win
She wants to be interested
She wants to get me
She throws like an angel is guiding her roll
She bounds ahead
"Throw doubles" she says egging me on
But she does not realizes that the die don't have the
      same numbers
And suddenly it is not a game
She won't let me resign
And as we finish she throws pieces into place
Wanting another

Sometimes it is hard to just let it be ..

Your There (5/31)

How I want to write you each day
Brilliant words
Do you know
You understand
How two birds make love in the air spiraling
    down
And separating before they die
Silence day
What it is
Upon my face to see
Your face upon my mind
Twisted time
See your face
Close, but not quite there
Like polar magnets dancing true
Me and you
Again I wish
I feel you now and wonder how
That connection lives
Through it all
I know your there
I feel you here
We make it hard
Love me well
Gone to hell
Each
Each
Love within reach
Brandish G-d
Have your peace
Remembering the well

45

Sometimes what is not said is more than what could ever be said.

Silence (6/05)

Don't talk any more
I can hear you from the distance
Your words fall hard
Like hail on a field of wheat
Names that you know I detest
Spew from your mouth
Like a sick child's vomit
Replete with your soul's venom
Tire yourself
See me wait and shield myself
Through your exquisite torrent
Of utter silence

Family

She knew how to just be with someone. She graced me with a visit that still brings a smile to my face...

Nana (7/84)

I went shopping for Nana today.
I bought shredded wheat and cottage cheese,
I hope she'll be pleased.

She's mighty old my nana is.
She almost spans this century,
She'll be loved eternally.

We often play cards together.
We tease around with everyone,
We always have some fun.

I expect Nana's flight tonight.
I wait anxiously all these hours,
I'll be there with flowers.

I love him through day and night...

Brother (8/84)

When I was born,
  You were my brother,
When you didn't want me,
  I was your brother.

When darkness came into your mind,
  You were my brother
Without understanding came another,
  You were my brother
When darkness came and took your mind,
  I was your brother.

When you fought the fight,
  You were my brother
When you made a deal and saw the dawn,
  You were my brother
And when the darkness comes again,
  I'll be your brother.

My daughter had just been conceived. It demarked two parts of my life. The knee in the curve. This poem came in the long dry spell and foretold of the key to rekindling my interest in writing.

The Past (3/90)

Ten years ago I had no question
No erring in my faith,
I'd travel five years into the past,
And correct all of fate's mistakes.

But in the intervening years,
I've worked so very hard,
At work and school and life itself,
It's fate I now applaud.

Other lives would surely benefit,
If I traveled 10 years into the past,
Am I greedy not to want to go?
Or am I settled with it at last?

The tooth fairy wrote to her each time she lost a tooth. This was the final note …

T.F. Final (10/01)

For years now, sweet Sammi, we didn't know if you
	knew,
With each new tooth, our love only grew.
It challenged our imagination and it became a game,
To leave a cool note that wouldn't be the same.
We almost got caught, many times over the years,
Sometimes silver dollars came very dear.
Across oceans, back to back, and far away miles,
Others helped, even Mickey, to keep a kid's smiles.
Now you have grown, the final one is here,
One last dollar and note, one happiness tear.
Remember the joy, the excitement and surprise,
Take a snapshot in your head of the look in your eyes.
You were a T.F. in training and didn't know that you'd
	learn,
To bring joy to your own child when it is your turn.

I do not know why I have not written more.
Maybe this Senryu sums it up.

Mom (4/17/2)

She is my hero,
Dedication to what's right,
Pure perseverance

My father's mother derogatorily called her the redhead or raytta. She had a hard life. I hope that she has found peace...

Raytta (6/02)

There is a woman who just died
I didn't always treat her right
Now it seems few have cried

She was my father's second wife
And got very little honor
Yet she made his life

Then he lied to her when they were wed
She never knew he was sick
Till his mind doth fled

The story goes, she tried to flee
But she had not heeded hers
And thus denied sanctuary

He'd say no to my overnights
Until he'd tell her about it
And she'd make it right

She'd shop food favs for the tummy
She would pay attention to me
And she'd play 500 rummy

My father's mother had some blame
But it got weird as I grew up
And never was again the same

After he died, it was by the next fall
She had alienated everyone
Till no one would call

We hadn't talked in nine plus years
And I wish I felt guilty
And shed her some tears

I hereby thank her and I'm glad
She was on this earth
For my behalf and that of my dad

~

A gift of G-d …

Sammi (5/03)

G-d watches over
As she becomes a woman
But still my baby

Sleeping (6/6/2)

She is so pretty
When she lays asleep in bed
Like winter's first snow

She was just sitting there doing homework. I looked up and said "wait, wait" and started writing ...

Sammi and I (10/03)

She sits besides me now
Not grown but wise and worn
Still a child but ready for her fair
Seems like yesterday we danced
We danced with abandon
Today is about homework and rules
Sleeping, eating and health
Hormonal waves and independence
She runs me down when she sees me
We smile and chit chat
We shared our defense
Now we must share our future
And find the space for us both to grow
Leaning less, forgiving more
Remembering always to love
Never looking back

Nana was turning 100. I wrote this for her party.
I read it aloud to everyone at the party ...

Autumn Leaves (12/03)

"Look at the colors" she says
Knowing that this autumn is like all those she has seen
Yet she finds wonder
And we find wonder
Not just in the autumns she has seen
But in the glimpse we get of what she sees
Nothing is old
All leaves find equanimity in her glance
All leaves show their brightest colors for her glance
Her smile and joy support each in their passage
Vying for but a second of attention
A quiet word
A game played out beneath sun and stars
Ultimately finding comfort with her mere presence
They linger as long as possible and then fall
All the while longing for another season with Nana

We had socialized by playing cards – thousands of games. When she passed, I knew what she would be doing …

Play Again (6/04)

Deal the hand
No blood around the table
Momentary gloating required
Come play with me
Three-handed, four-handed
What is around that table?
Laughter, love

One more game
One more hand
Don't go just yet
The tournament has just begun

I know they are holding your spot
Go on then
Play one for me
        And hold my spot
Till we might play again...

Self

~

Contrasts. The night was always crazy time for me.
The morning brought new hope and order.

Confusion (2/84)

Confusion and love and lust,
Tonight my life will hurt,
But the morning will bring the sun,
How does my life go on?

Intensity and love and solitude,
My love is for the asking,
But alone is our ultimate truth,
Regardless, life must be good.

Purpose and love and pain,
Awakening is my standard,
No more is what we want,
Is anything worth suffering?

Death and love and life,
I will always try my best,
But we are only human,
Alas, such is life.

What do we have to fear?

Pool (6/01)

He was already 7 and couldn't swim in the pool,
      "Relegate him" they said, oh the swimmers
      were cruel.
To the small pool he went, some kids were there too,
      He splashed and sat on the bottom, with
      nothing else to do.

He tried to swim anyway, and sometimes they fussed,
      But down he went, no unconditional trust.
They finally gave up, he couldn't be taught,
      But then on his own, he had a very bright
      thought.

"I know how to sit, on the bottom of pool,
      All this time I have just been a silly old fool".
"If I swim" he was thinking, he told himself so,
      "And then I sink I'll go back to what I
      already know",

He learned to swim, but that's not the end of the story,
      He somehow created a lesson that lessens
      your worry.
What's the worst that can happen, oh brave little rule
      You probably know how to sit, at the bottom
      of the pool.

He said find some pictures from your youth. See there where the smile and brightness was no longer apparent. Now we must work to get it back.

Prize (9/01)

He knows there's a prize
The light in his eyes
Before he dies

There when he was born, gone when he was 5,
     Even though he lived, he was just less alive,
Wonder was lost, leaving existence to thrive.

His character was relatively flawed,
     Compared to the other, they needed the rod,
But a hero he became and they had to applaud.

As in War and Peace, he became a thinking person,
     He knew his life could have been a worse one.
He watched all around him the unending destruction.

Is there G-d and is He just?
     Is there more to life than pleasure and lust?
Is dogma and ritual just iron with rust?

He was moral and responsible but didn't really care,
     He formalized his garden by reading Voltaire,
He built a shelf and the unresolved went there.

He found reasons to get up and live life,
     A hard work ethic, a career and even a wife,
But he couldn't escape his earlier strife.

In biblical terms he hardened his heart,
     But the skills that he learned let him play any
     part,
And the smile and wonder became a lost art.

He knows there's a prize
The light in his eyes
Before he dies

The shape preceded the content. I had postulated from early in my life that you make rules with your heart and execute with your head because at times of stress it was easy for your heart to get distracted.

Heart & Mind (5/02)

It flows like a mighty river through life's terrain
The smallest rain can change its course
Bain and virtue, it generates energy
It meanders often, changing course
Evolution was its only creator
Clouds and sun affect it
Many use and divert it
It gives happiness
It is forever
Heart
Mind
It is finite
It develops things
It may choose to hide
Only time takes its toll
It is planned and manufactured
Its plan doesn't include deviation
It is a vessel defined by its content
Only an earthquake can break its stride
It stands like a road and leads to the destination

Part of my poem-a-day collection. These exercises in minimalism helped me focus the thoughts of the day and helped sparked my desire to write.

Talk to yourself (3/02)

Decide with your heart
Only live life with your head
Hearts react too much

Pragmatism (5/02)

Truth is transient
You must start from where you are
And expect nothing

Who is Right (5/02)

Nobody is wrong,
G-d is an abstract painting,
You see what you want

Battles (5/02)

Passion for beliefs
Pick the few most important
Or lose all of them

Candide (7/02)

Thinking's dangerous,
Voltaire said "tend your garden",
Accomplish something.

When I was young I prayed for something and got it but the price … Oh the price. I felt as if it were a monkey's paw. So I stopped asking G-d for anything and just thanked Him for what I had instead.

Morning Prayer (8/03)

I lower myself to my knees and pray
Some prayers I am afraid to say

I thank G-d for all I have
I do not ask and that is sad
But find the thanks that says it all

For family and loved ones
For my personal growth
Where I still must find the path

For my job and house and bed
For teaching me about patience
When continued lessons are destined

For my frailties and challenges
For the strength given to persevere
Because life needs dark and light

For that elusive feeling that you know
For feelings of desire and need
Even tempered with insecurity

I thank G-d for all I have
I find the words and thankful of that too
And experience peace before the day

I rise up from my knees and pray
A prayer of grace for this new day

It is hard to not be defensive. It is hard to truly forgive. Retribution and penance between people is the fodder for festering discontent.

Forgiveness (10/9)

Forgiveness is a trait attributed to gods
It is easy for mere humans to give
Actions and reactions appealed and repealed
But less likely I am afraid for to live

Begrudge and resent, insidious brothers
Time has no mark on their souls
Why can we conceive as if we were gods
But lead our lives as if we are fools

Pray thee Lord lend me Your will
For I wish to forgive one and all
Their repentance should not enter my thoughts
But their hearts should release me from thrall

We were together a long time. I did not feel. I did not write. I take responsibility …

Chalice (10/03)

She said in the mists that my words were sad
I used it as an excuse
Like a knight withdrawing from battle
From a broken heart
Some asked me why I remained in that world
I had no answers then
I was taken by Voltaire's last chapter
Do and do not think
Hardship bred restraint as chain mail for my heart
Complicity muting mind and soul
Fugue as a rule instead of exception
Where din occupied awareness
I complied
No, indeed I needed the void
But it was hollow

The blame is upon me
I intended to turn sword to plowshare and tend
Instead, instead life was like a padded room
Slowly turned inward by my perception
Perceptions of her selfish acts
Heart scarred by the cut of a thousand knives
Still no words came from me
No rhythm from my soul
No engagement in war or play

Apathy ruled the day
I walked a line of shimmering calm and calamitous
    dread
Perfect storms where the work seemed pallid
Through it all the chalice was there
Keeping a small spark lit
The nectar of a child's love
Reminded me of the light
Reminded me of relativity
Reminded me of capacity
My soul drank more deeply than one might
Slowly cracking open my heart
I awaited the dawn

Now, I have awoken
Time has passed
I wish to be better and venture forth on quest
With new arms and mail meant for thought
I feel the strength and ability
To both think and do
Armed, aware and willing to risk all
I believe in G-d and spirit
I conceive of better and shall be so
Learning forgiveness
New ways to lay siege to truth
Never to withdraw again
Let the words come
Giving me a chance
To love

~

Emotionlessness haunts me. I can express my feelings with words and poetry but not very easily with my body.

Robotic Flu (5/04)

Morning again and
I am eating light today
Brought to my knees by robotic flu
Terminally tempered or so I thought
What will it take to show them?
Do I not care?
Can I not try harder?
Love is bound by history
The future is rife with Houdini-esque tricks
To set one free

The leap of faith.

As if (5/04)

As if
As if it were
As if reality were my dreams
To live
To give as if
To share as if we were
Overcome the past
Something that will last
Believe with your soul
As if

Acknowledgments

Great thanks to all the people who reviewed this book: Sandra Himelstein, Tony Barreca, and Nausheen Omar.

Great love to my family for their everlasting patience and support.

About The Author

Mark Himelstein has been writing poetry since 1983.

In his day job, Mark is currently the President and CEO of Heavenstone, Inc. a software development and management consulting firm (www.heavenstone.us). He just released a book through his company on software management entitled *100 Questions to Ask Your Software Organization*.

Mark earned a Bachelor of Science in both Computer Science and Mathematics from Wilkes College in Wilkes-Barre, Pennsylvania. Mark earned his Masters Degree in Computing Science from the University of California at Davis/Livermore. Mark holds four patents and has published a number of technical papers.

Mark lives in Saratoga, CA with his daughter, Sammi.